# SEA in my Cells

Laura Alary & Andrea Blinick

pajamapress

**First published in Canada and the United States in 2025**

Text copyright © 2025 Laura Alary
Illustration copyright © 2025 Andrea Blinick
This edition copyright © 2025 Pajama Press Inc.
This is a first edition.
10 9 8 7 6 5 4 3 2 1

All rights reserved. No part of this publication may be reproduced, stored in a retrieval system or transmitted, in any form or by any means, without the prior written consent of the publisher or a licence from The Canadian Copyright Licensing Agency (Access Copyright). For an Access Copyright licence, visit www.accesscopyright.ca or call toll free 1.800.893.5777.

www.pajamapress.ca    winfo@pajamapress.ca

 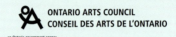 

The publisher gratefully acknowledges the support of the Canada Council for the Arts and the Ontario Arts Council for its publishing program. We acknowledge the financial support of the Government of Canada through the Canada Book Fund (CBF) for our publishing activities.

**Library and Archives Canada Cataloguing in Publication**

Title: Sea in my cells / Laura Alary & Andrea Blinick.
Names: Alary, Laura, author. | Blinick, Andrea, 1979- illustrator.
Description: First edition.
Identifiers: Canadiana 20240501454 | ISBN 9781772783421 (hardcover)
Subjects: LCSH: Hydrologic cycle—Juvenile literature. | LCGFT: Picture books. | LCGFT: Informational works.
Classification: LCC GB848 .A43 2025 | DDC j551.48—dc23

**Publisher Cataloging-in-Publication Data (U.S.)**

Names: Alary, Laura, author | Blinick, Andrea, 1979-, illustrator.
Title: Sea in my cells / Laura Alary & Andrea Blinick.
Description: First edition. | Toronto, Ontario : Pajama Press ; La Vergne, TN : Distributed in the U.S. by Ingram Publisher Services, 2025. | Summary: "Describes, in free verse, how the water cycle shapes our planet--from cloud, to sea, to refreshing glass of water, to cell"—Provided by publisher.
Identifiers: ISBN 978-1-77278-342-1 (hardcover)
Subjects: LCSH: Hydrologic cycle–Juvenile literature. | Weather–Juvenile literature. | Water–Juvenile literature. | Nature–Juvenile literature. | Health—Juvenile literature. | BISAC: JUVENILE NONFICTION / Science & Nature / General. | JUVENILE NONFICTION / Science & Nature / Earth Sciences / Water (Oceans, Lakes, etc.). | JUVENILE NONFICTION / Science & Nature / Earth Sciences / Weather. | JUVENILE NONFICTION / Health & Daily Living / General.
Classification: LCC GB848.A323 2025 | DDC 551.48– dc23

Original art created digitally
Cover and book design—Simin Dewji

Printed in China

Pajama Press Inc.
11 Davies Avenue, Suite 103, Toronto, Ontario Canada, M4M 2A9

Distributed in Canada by UTP Distribution
5201 Dufferin Street Toronto, Ontario Canada, M3H 5T8

Distributed in the U.S. by Publishers Group West
1 Ingram Blvd. La Vergne, TN 37086, USA

Come sit in the shade.
It is so hot and
you've been playing hard.
Does the breeze feel cool
on your damp skin?

See how your dog licks your arm with her pink tongue.
Your sweat is salty like the sea.

When you are this thirsty there is nothing better than a tall glass of water.

You need water because you are water! Your body is filled with it.

Why don't you slosh when you run? Because all that water is held in your cells.

Everything alive—including you—is made of cells.
They come in different shapes and sizes,
but they are all full of water.

In that water float even smaller parts that make your body work.

So drink up.
You need to put the sea in your cells.

But wait—the sea?
In your glass of water?
How can that be?

Not so long ago,
the sun shone on the ocean
and warmed it.

Wind swept over the water
and gathered moisture into the air,
the way the breeze dries the sweat
from your flushed face.

The moisture became clouds
which sailed
over the ocean,
over the land,
and up the hills where the air was cool.

Inside those cooling clouds,
mist turned to drops—too heavy to hold.
They fell as raindrops,
round and playful,
landing with a splash!

The rain became puddles,
which trickled into rivers,
flowed into lakes,
and seeped into the ground,
held between layers of rock.

But the water didn't stay there.
Some was pumped into pipes.
It rushed along for miles

until at last it gushed
from your tap
into your glass.

Do you see?

From sea to clouds.

From clouds to rain.

From rain to lake.

From lake to glass.

Water is a shape-shifter.

Take a big gulp.
Can you taste the sea?
Imagine it filling up
every thirsty cell.

But the water doesn't stop with you either.

All day long you
>breathe it out
>>sweat it out
>>>cry it out
>>>>pee it out!

Where does it go?

Back to the air
  to the ground
    to the lakes
      to the rivers
        to the sea.

All the water that is
is all that ever was.
So the water in your glass
has been many things
in many places
at many times.

Maybe it was once
an iceberg,
or mist in a rain forest.
Maybe it fell as snowflakes
on a woolly mammoth,
or was lapped up
by a thirsty Stegosaurus!

Swallow those last few drops.
Do you feel as cool as a cloud?
As fresh as a raindrop?
As playful as a river?
As wild as the ocean?

You're ready to run again.
You have the sea in your cells.

## — Author's Note —

Breathe into your hand. Does your palm feel damp? That's water. Water is inside you, in your breath, your cells, and your tears, which are salty like the sea. Water is all around you too, in many forms: clouds and rain, ponds and puddles, dew and frost, rivers and glaciers. It is the ice that cools your drink, the frozen lake you skate on, the snowflakes you catch on your tongue, and the steam that whistles from your teakettle.

Water shapes our planet. It pounds rocky beaches into sand, sculpts mountains and valleys, seeps into the smallest cracks and breaks apart boulders as it freezes and thaws. And it is water that brings the earth to life. Life began in the sea. The first living things were bacteria that floated in the ocean. From these simple cells, over billions of years, came every kind of plant and animal. Many of them lived in the sea, and those that moved onto land had to bring a bit of the ocean with them. For example, reptiles were able to spread out into dry places because their eggs had tough outsides that kept the watery insides safe from the sun. You could say they had the sea in their shells!

All the water on earth is all there ever was, and all there ever will be. So we need to take good care of it. The next time you pour a glass of water, take a moment to think about all the wonderful things this life-giving shape-shifter does.

Before you take that first sip, say thank you.

—Laura Alary